101 Tips for Families Surviving Absence or Deployment

Megan Egerton
&
John Willman

Please Read

The authors have done their best to present accurate and up-to-date information in this book, but they cannot guarantee that the information is correct or will suit your particular situation. This book is sold with the understanding that the publisher and authors are not engaged in rendering legal, accounting, counselling or any other professional services. If expert assistance is required, the services of a competent professional should be sought.

Copyright 2009 Egerton Graham Consulting
ISBN 978-0-9811436-0-6
Version 1.1

Author: Megan Egerton Graham

Design and Illustration: John Willman

Published by Egerton Graham Consulting
www.egertongrahamconsulting.com

For Cynthia, Jake and Justin. Without them we would be lost. Thank you for all of your love support and patience

Forward

This book was created to support family members through any and all extended absences of a significant member of your family. All of the tips and suggestions have been tried and/ or tested either by our family or other families experiencing absences. Enjoy reading all of the tips but don't feel as though you have to complete each one. Think of this guide as a recipe book, some recipes will work perfectly for your family and some recipes your family would never even want to sample. The intent of the book is to make the absence easier and give your family the tools to thrive during your their absence.

Get Organized

"If you can organize your kitchen, you can organize your life"
— *Louis Parrish*

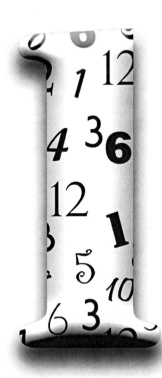

Being organized will help you be and feel more in control of your life in general.

Suggestions

- Keep a grocery list on the fridge so you can remember what you need to restock
- Create a family calendar of events and dates of departure and return
- File cards monthly and put on postage so that you can easily write and mail it
- Buy in bulk
- Maintain "To Do" lists
- Organize clothes, lunches, etc. the night before

Simplify your life

"Everything should be made as simple as possible but not simpler"
— *Albert Einstein*

Reduce number of tasks you do in day.

Take on things that are important and bring you happiness and reduce the number of things that add frustration, stress and upset.

Suggestions

- Tell family and friends that during this absence you are going to take on less and try to simplify things
- If watering your plants if just another burden – give them to a friend
- If mowing your lawn is too stressful – ask someone to help or pay someone else to do it
- Let go of tasks that other people would be able to easily take on

Re-assess priorities

"At the end of your life, you will never regret not having passed one more test, not winning one more verdict or not closing one more deal. You will regret time not spent with a husband, friend, a child or parent"
— Barbara Bush

Assess what is important to you, gives your life meaning and what provides you a sense of fulfillment.

Suggestions

• Make a list of all of the "Have To's", "Want To's", "Don't Need To's"

• Ask yourself "If it doesn't get done what are the consequences?"

• Let people know what your priorities are so that they can support you

• Before doing major tasks or taking on large projects or commitments ask yourself the important questions like: Will this bring me happiness? Is this important? Will this enhance my life

Short term goals

"Many people have a wrong idea of what constitutes real happiness. It is not obtained through self gratification, but through fidelity to a worthy purpose"
— *Helen Keller*

Focusing on the things that need to, and can get done will give you a sense of accomplishment and increased level of confidence. Make your goals short and realistic.

Suggestions

- Add "2" onto whatever time line you have created for yourself (2mins to get it done would be 4mins, 2 days to accomplish it would be 4 days, etc.)
- Forgive yourself if it doesn't get accomplished
- Reward yourself when you accomplish a short term goal (have an extra long bath, order pizza, read a book)

Long term goals

"Nothing contributes so much to tranquilize the mind as a steady purpose — a point on which the soul may fix its intellectual eye"
— *Mary Wollstonecraft Shelley*

Having a long term goal

to reach gives you another reason to get up in the morning, dreams to strive for and a focus to work towards.

Suggestions

• Share your long term goal with your family or have the family create one together (i.e. family holiday, pool, weight loss)

• When everyone is aware of the goal(s) they can better support you

• Write your long term goals down and post them where everyone can see them

Time with friends

"Lots of people want to ride with you in the limo, but what you want is someone who will take the bus with you when the limo breaks down."

— Oprah Winfrey

Sharing time with people who love and care about you helps to alleviate the sense of being alone.

Suggestions

• Spend time with people who energize and enrich your life

• Attempt to see friends and family in person instead of on the phone – you get a break and a much greater sense of connectedness

• Join a club, organization or evening class you've always wanted to

• Get a partner to go to the gym with

• Make spending time with a friend(s) or family part of your weekly routine

Keep busy

"People who know how to employ themselves, always find leisure moments, while those who do nothing are forever in a hurry"
— *Jeanne-Marie Roland*

Sitting at home is not going to distract your mind from your worries and fears and it won't give you a sense of purpose.

Suggestions

- Take on tasks and work that is meaningful to you
- Take on an activity of hobby that you have always wanted to do
- Volunteer at your child's school
- Join a support group and find out what you could do in the community
- Choose tasks or activities that are going to lift your spirits not become an overwhelming burden

Laugh everyday

"The human race has one really effective weapon, and that is laughter"
– *Mark Twain*

With laughter comes the restoration of hope.

When you are able to laugh each day you are able to shake off your stress and worries, if only for a few minutes.

Suggestions

- Rent funny movies
- Read funny books
- Get your children to tell you some jokes
- Watch something or someone silly on www.youtube.com
- Get a daily tear off calendar with funny sayings or cartoons of funny happenings or happy moments.

Pamper yourself

"I define comfort as self-acceptance. When we finally learn that self-care begins and ends with ourselves, we no longer demand sustenance and happiness from others."
— *Jennifer Louden*

In order to properly care for your family you need to be well rested and taken care of too! Routinely setting aside time to do something to maintain your well-being is essential.

Suggestions

- Go for a massage
- Get a manicure or pedicure
- Get your hair done
- Go shopping and only buy yourself something
- Get dressed up and go out for a fancy dinner
- Attend a sports event, buy the "good" tickets, and use valet
- Remind yourself how hard you've been working and reward yourself regularly

Journal daily

"The act of putting pen to paper encourages pause for thought, this in turn makes us think more deeply about life, which helps us regain our equilibrium."
— *Norbet Platt*

Writing your thoughts and feelings is cathartic. It is a great way to express your thoughts feelings and the daily life happenings. It is also an excellent way of keeping your loved one in touch with what is important in your world and what you are feeling and thinking.

Suggestions

- Journal your thoughts daily
- Write as often as you like
- Don't think of it as a burden but as a way of taking time for you
- Write 2 lines or 200 lines – whatever you feel like
- You could send the journals weekly or monthly as a good way of keeping your absent family member in touch and up to date
- Attach pictures or ticket stubs, etc.

"Trouble is a part of your life and if you don't share it, you don't give the person who loves you enough chance to love you enough."

— *Anon*

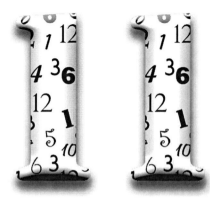

Being honest and open will provide you and your family with immeasurable comfort. By sharing your fears and worries you will feel less alone, more understood and the same goes for them!

Suggestions

- Share at appropriate times and when you have adequate time to talk things through
- Make a "Things We Can Change / Things We Can't Change" list. Recognizing what you can and can't control will help you to put perspective on your fears or worries and determine how much energy you should devote to them
- Have the family write down one fear or worry on a piece of paper and then put it in a container. Each person chooses a piece of paper and then you discuss that worry together. Once you have talked about it you rip up the piece of paper and throw it out.

> "The best smell in the world
> is that man that you love"
> — *Jennifer Aniston*

Smell

Familiar scents can be incredibly comforting, trigger happy memories and give you a sense of security.

Suggestions

- Cook a favourite meal
- Use their favourite deoderant
- Put a face cloth in a ziplock with their most often used scent, soap, etc. (Sealing it will prevent the scent from fading quickly).
- Familiar smell can be soothing and comforting
- This can work both ways – you could have their smell and they could have yours
- When you send a package give the paper or item a spray

Play a board game

"It is not about how much time you spend together, it is about the time you do spend together"

— *Anon*

13

Games bring everyone together and can often be good ways of indirectly approaching subjects that are sensitive or difficult to talk about.

Suggestions

• Buy the game 'Jenga' and then open it up and write questions on the tiles (When each tile/block is pulled out they have to answer that question)
• To motivate reluctant players you could offer the winner a day or week off a particular chore!
• Choose any game that will bring your family together for some fun and laughter
• Give each family member a chance to choose the game
• Set aside a specific time to play and put away all cell phones, MP3 plyers etc.

Create a new recipe

"Home cooking is a
catalyst that brings
people together"
— *Marion Cunningham*

Food can be comforting and cooking together can bring people closer together and initiate conversation.

Suggestions

- Add different ingredients to a favourite recipe (i.e. chocolate chips to pancake batter)
- Make a While You Were Away cookie and send them
- Create a While You Were Away recipe book
- Bake favourite desserts each week or month to celebrate surviving another week or month
- Grocery shop together - you'll get help with groceries and plan fun meals at the same time

Movie night

"Every time I go to a movie, it's magic, no matter what the movie's about."
— *Steven Spielberg*

Have a night each week that is devoted to watching a TV show or movie together.

Suggestions

- Choose shows or movies carefully – think about what emotions or moods they might evoke
- Make it special by getting popcorn or a special treat to go with the movie
- Give your family 100% of you by not answering the phone, emails, etc.
- Make this night a part of your routine
- If you have a busy schedule, each week consult with your family or friends for the best day/night to have it

Take 15mins

"To keep a lamp burning,
we have to keep putting
oil in it"

— *Mother Teresa*

Making time for yourself will leave you in a better state to look after those around you.

Suggestions

- Read something fun, light or interesting
- Take a long bath
- Take the phone off the hook
- Put a sign up on your door that says "Come back in 30mins"
- Set up an auto-reply on your email
- Remember that if there isn't a gun being held to your head, you don't need to deal with it immediately!

Accept Emotions

"My recipe for dealing with anger and frustration: set the kitchen timer for twenty minutes, cry, rant, and rave, and at the sound of the bell, simmer down and go about business as usual"

— *Phyllis Diller*

Don't let emotions like resentment, anger or frustration consume you but accept that they are real and that you are only human.

Suggestions

• Vent in appropriate places at appropriate times when possible.
• Keep a journal and let it out!
• Share your thoughts, resentments, anger with a friend
• Do a strenuous workout
• Punch a pillow
• Wait a full 24 hours before expressing your feelings to your absent significant other
• Write an email but don't send it until the next day

Exercise regularly

"It is important for a person to remain healthy and sound because a healthy mind dwells in a healthy body"

— *Rigveda*

Exercises increases our ability to cope with stressful situations, reduces tension and helps maintain our overall health and feelings of wellness.

Suggestions

- Use your local gym
- Buy a treadmill or piece of exercise equipment
- Take a walk every night
- Make exercise a family affair – run to the park together, bike together, go swimming
- Get an exercise partner of friend so that you can motivate each other
- Set some specific fitness goals

Responsibilities

"Responsibility is the price
of greatness"

— *Winston Churchill*

With an absence may come additional responsibilities to take on, perhaps temporarily. Distribute household chores fairly and give everyone a chance to demonstrate their ability to shine.

Suggestions

- Create a new 'chore chart' with the entire family before the person departs
- Distribute chores/responsibilities evenly and fairly
- Give rewards or incentives for family members when they complete their tasks
- Praise often and reduce criticism to a minimum
- Assign tasks according to the time they take rather than the number of them

Celebrate change

"Realize that change is here, embrace it. Don't just try to survive. Take the challenge to thrive"

— *Melanie Sojourner*

Take time to look at the things in your life that have changed during the absence and celebrate the positive changes that have happened to your family.

Suggestions

- Model the acceptance of change
- Use changes to bring out strengths in family members
- Make a chart of "Things I'd Like To Change", "Things I Want to Stay The Same", "Things to do together as a family" before they leave and when they return
- Talk about a past big change and focus on a lot of positives that came out of it
- Have a special celebration, with a dinner or night out, when there has been a significant or positive change

Write letters

"It does me good to write a letter which is not a response to a demand, a gratuitous letter, so to speak, which has accumulated in me like waters of a reservoir"

— *Henry Miller*

Write letters to each other often, they will help you to bridge gaps, connect with each other and make the reintegration upon the return much easier.

Suggestions

- Pre-address and put correct postage on envelopes for each other before leaving
- Get sectioned file folder and categorize by month and place cards for all occasions, celebrations, anniversaries, etc. so that each month you can easily acknowledge special occassions
- Start each letter with "I miss you because…"
- End each letter with "I love you because…"
- Avoid making letters all about the things you don't like or are having difficulty with
- Make sure you have the correct mailing address before they leave

Display photos

"A true photograph need not be explained, nor can it be contained in words"

— *Ansel Adams*

Nothing captures moments and memories better than family photos.

Suggestions

- Take special family photos before leaving and have them hung or placed throughout the house in high trafic areas
- Put different photos in every room
- Use photos from a variety of occassions, places, year, etc.
- Create a collage as a screen saver
- Send an email with the picture of the day
- Buy an electronic key chain or frame that can cycle through a lot of special, fun pictures

"A library is a hospital for
the mind"

— *Anonymous*

Losing yourself in a book or taking the time to read to your children is a great way to reduce stress and relax.

Suggestions

- Read every day or evening to your children
- Choose to read books to your children that will echo their thoughts and feelings and books that they can relate to
- Choose books that are interesting, make you laugh and that you can get 'lost' in
- Start a book club or trade with friends
- Send the book you read with personal notes for them to read as they read the book

Ask for help

"Plant a seed of friendship; reap a bouquet of happiness"
— *Lois L. Kauffman*

Asking other people for support, advice or assistance can not only get you the help that you need but it can also let others feel useful.

Suggestions

• Ask members of your family to contribute to meals

• Ask for someone to make a weekly check-in call for the sole purpose of seeing how you are and what you need and listen to a little bit about what you could do with less of!

• Ask someone you trust to drive your children to an event or an activity (you could also set up a schedule of supporting each other which would give you both a sense of usefulness and time to rest)

• Ask for help during special occasions or events (bringing something with them, coming over earlier to help, having someone else do the photos and filming, etc.)

Be flexible

"Success is not built on success. It's built on failure. It's built on frustration. Sometimes its built on catastrophe."

— *Sumner Redstone*

Change happens daily and, good or bad, these changes can significantly impact your life. Try to stay as flexible as possible with your expectations, routines and demands – both on yourself and those around you. Being flexible doesn't mean you give up consistency – it means you leave room for error.

Suggestions

- When making appointments give yourself twice the time you used to
- Don't maintain tight time lines when you don't have to
- Always give yourself an extra 30mins to get anywhere. Tell people that you will be there between a certain 30min time frame so that if something comes up you are able to deal with it and still won't be late
- If your plans change think first about all the benefits to the change and it will help you to feel less frustrated

Hide notes

> "In a great romance, each person plays a roll that the other really likes"
>
> — *Elizabeth Ashley*

26

Finding hidden notes unexpectedly can brighten your day and help brighten someone else's.

Suggestions

• Take an entire block of Post-It notes or a small note pad and write messages to your loved ones and leave them all over the house.

• Remember seasons change and so do clothes so you could hide one in a flip flop and another in a winter coat

• The notes don't need to be long but could be famous quotes, a simple, "I love you" or "I miss you" or "Remember the time when we…" or something that you know will bring a smile to their face.

Be patient

> "The two most powerful warriors are patience and time"
> — *Leo Nikolaevich Tolstoy*

Try to keep in mind that there is always someone who is worse off than you are. Be patient with your children ~ their ups and downs and with yourself. Don't expect to turn into a superhero, just do what you can with what you have.

Suggestions

• Try not to react to situations, comments, people etc. immediately

• Allow for others to make mistakes, say or do the wrong thing, not understand, etc.

• Before speaking or responding to anything count to ten in your head or ask yourself if this is thing that is worth expending energy on

• Listen to not only what someone is saying but what they are trying to tell you

• Take a long bath or do breathing exercises

• Rate yourself (with each situation being a new opportunity to improve your "score" in how patient you can be)

• When you feel yourself becoming impatient, say it

Create a door sign

"The time to repair the roof
is when the sun is shinning"

— *John F. Kennedy*

Everyone needs a place and some space of their own to unwind and be alone with their thoughts.

Suggestions

• Put up a sign on your door that says to everyone you need some space
• Everyone in your family needs time to reflect, unwind, be alone and have some privacy but as with everything, there needs to be a good balance
• Set ground rules:
  • The sign can only go up once a day
  • If the sign is up for longer than the maximum time allowed then anyone in the family can ask you why and with a good explanation you can get an "extension"
  • Using the sign should not replace talking things out with others

Be honest

"Integrity is telling myself the truth. And honesty is telling the truth to other people"

— *Spencer Johnson*

If we look back on our own childhoods, I am sure we would find that some of our largest upsets were when our parents were not honest with us.

Suggestions

• Tell the truth but be selective with the amount of information you give (depending on age of the child)

• Be honest about how you are feeling with your children – this honesty may spark some of their own too and meaningful discussions could alleviate a lot of stress and worry

• Ask people to be honest with you in return.

• Keep a journal of 'raw' and honest thoughts and feelings you are experiencing

• Make sure you are balancing positive and negative remarks when being honest with someone

• Ask yourself – Would I want them to tell me?

Accept it!

"You can't change the weather, only how you dress for it"

— *Megan Egerton Graham*

Look at what you can change and don't be a salmon swimming up stream. Make sure you know what the things are that you can't change and focus on the ones that you can do something about.

Suggestions

• Make a list of all the things you want to change and then highlight the ones that you can change and circle the ones you are just going to have to accept

• Share your thoughts, ideas and perspectives with others

• Create a motto for yourself about acceptance and change

• Each day, before getting out of bed, think about one thing you are not happy about yet cannot change and think of a benefit that could arise of it being the way it is

• Find humour in the things that you are forced to endure or deal with

"People need to be listened to often as much as they need food. And if you'll take time time to feed them, you'll create some fabulous friendships."

— *Sean Covey*

O pen and honest communication is essential and will help you and your family to not only manage, in your loved one's absence, but thrive.

Suggestions

• Dinner conversation cards are another way to get the lines of communication going. Put a card under each person's plate with a question on it. A further motivation, if necessary, could be that the person who has the best answer doesn't have to do dishes or even clear up.

• Make your own family board game after Monopoly or The Game of Life that is all about you and your family. If you are extra creative you can even make your own game pieces. It will get you talking about the pitfalls and bonuses of your lives together

• Each person has to tell the family about a good and a bad thing that happened in their day during dinner (you could also threaten no dessert if they don't share).

Memory box

"To look backward for a while is to refresh the eye, to restore it, and to render it the more fit for its prime function of looking forward."

— *Margaret Fairless Barber*

A memory box during the absence is a good way to start opening up the lines of communication upon their return – each item will tell a story.

Suggestions
• Save a shoebox or buy a pre-decorated box or go to a craft store and buy one that needs decorating and make that a project that you do together.
• Inside the box your family can put in pictures, ticket stubs, awards from school, report cards, postcards, birthday cards, etc.
• Record the time and date of the items using post-it notes or write on the back of things to remind yourself about a funny incident or story that goes along with the memory
• Ask family and friends for contributions to the box too to get a wide range of perspectives on the time they have been away

Family night

"The best thing you can give children, next to good habits, are good memories."

— *Unknown*

Spending time as a family is essential and will help to reduce the sense of loneliness or isolation some people may feel.

Suggestions

- Schedule onto a calendar for everyone to spend time together
- Play a video game of your children's choice with them
- Go for ice cream or some dessert once a week together
- Go bowling or play mini-golf together once a month – choose any activity, the important thing is that you are doing it together
- Attend a community event together
- Walk the dog together or go to the park

Screen calls

"Life is now… this day, this hour… and is probably the only experience of the kind one is to have."

— *Charles Macomb and Flandrau*

The phone is not always your friend.

Phone calls can often be bothersome and do not add any value to your day. Some phone calls can even add to your stress levels.

Suggestions

- Choose dinner as the time you commit to not having any phone conversations
- Live by the 'mantra' – "If it is important, they'll call back". By doing this you are teaching your family about priorities and putting things into their proper perspective.
- Get an answering service or machine
- Turn off cell phones
- Set the "no-phone time" before they leave so they know when not to call or have a ring code so you know it is them (ex: 2 rings, hang up and call right back)

Say no

"Discipline is remembering what you want"

— *David Campbell*

Don't let the guilt you may feel about your family missing a significant member be replaced with the word "yes" when under other circumstances you would have definitely have said "No!".

Suggestions

• Find ways that you are comfortable in saying "no" to people

• Ask yourself if your significant other was there what they would say

• Set clear limits that have been established as a family so there are no misunderstandings – it is easier to say no when you have talked about expectations and consequences beforehand

• Make a list of all the things that are essential to do, the things that are important and then say no to things that aren't on those two lists

Set limits

"Many things which cannot be overcome when they are to gether, yield themselves up when take little by little."

— *Plutarch*

36

Letting friends and family know what your limits are and following through on maintaining those limits can make your life much easier when you have a loved one away.

Suggestions

- Talk about expectations prior to the person leaving
- Set up clear expectations and responsibilities for everyone in your family
- Let children know what your limits are by consequencing behaviour consistently, fairly and in a timely manner
- Let friends and family know your what your limitations are in advance (whenever possible) in regards to evenings out, commitments, celebrations or visiting
- Ask children, friends and family about what their limits are too

Create new routines

"I watch the Indy 500, and I was thinking that if they left earlier they wouldn't have to go so fast."

— *Steven Wright*

With an important family member absent there will be some changes in routine — some for the better and some that you will count the days until they come back so it can change back!

Suggestions

- Set up a routine with your family and ask for their input
- Look at what makes life easier for all of you
- Set realistic expectations for your family and yourself (especially about extracurricular activities, driving commitments, etc.
- With routine comes a sense of comfort and particularly that helps people to thrive in times of stress — be consistent and keep to it as much as possible
- Adjust the routine after a few weeks if needed so it supports everyone as much as possible

Special traditions

"Your children need your presence more than your presents"

— *Rev. Jessie Jackson*

Ask your family what traditions or family rituals they want to keep while your loved one is away and commit to keeping these in place as they are an important part of your family life. These traditions or unique family rituals help to provide a sense of cohesion and normalcy.

Suggestions

• Get out the calendar with your family and mark any days they feel are special and would want to celebrate or commemorate

• Talk about things that your family routinely does (night or morning routines, ways of greeting each other or saying good-bye, sayings they have, etc.) that they would like to continue

• Include the absent family member by referring to him/her or having a picture up (ex. If you always kissed before leaving the house then put a picture up by the door and kiss it on the way out)

People that support you

"Your wealth is where
your friends are."

—— *Plautus*

Make a list, with your family, of people that love and support you. When you commit to making a list, you are taking the time to think about all the people in your life that you count on for love and support.

Suggestions

- This list should be made up of people that you are comfortable asking for help from and who you know would enjoy giving you some extra help or support
- Create a list of people that are close by and people that are a phone call away
- Keep the list in a convenient location (fridge, by the phone, in your cell phone directory, at work, in the car, etc.)
- Let people know that they are on this list
- Make sure your family is aware of the list as they may need it too!
- Put a copy of the list in your child's backpack or agenda
- Make sure you update contact information with your work, children's school, etc.

Praise your children

"If you want your children to improve, let them overhear the nice things you say about them to others."

— *Haim Ginott*

Make it a daily habit to praise your children each day. They need encouragement like a plant needs water. The praise should be genuine, thoughtful and specific.

Suggestions

- Leave notes under their pillow or in their lunches that tell them you are proud of them
- Be specific about what exactly you are proud of or impressed by or amazed by
- Before anyone leaves in the morning tell them one specific thing you admire about them
- Before leaving the dinner table everyone has to say one positive thing about someone in their family
- Tuck your children into bed no matter how old they are, they will enjoy hearing your voice tell them something loving or encouraging just before sleeping

Listen

"If you want your
children to improve,
let them overhear the
nice things you say
about them to others."

— *Haim Ginott*

Let your family know you really hear what they are saying.

Suggestions

• Anytime you are listening pretend that someone is going to ask you word for word what they just said and for an interpretation of what they meant

• Make time to listen so that your family feels like you really heard what they were saying and weren't rushed

• Set aside time each day to have a conversation with your family where you make a point of listening 75% of the time and only talking 25%

• Turn off the radio or TV and tell them that you want all of your focus to be on them

• When they are finished try to give a summary back to them of what they heard (ex. So what I think you just said was that…)

• Unless there is a dire emergency do not let other tasks distract you from your goal – to listen

• Do not multitask – listening is your only job!

Plan an 'unbirthday'

"There is nothing better than birthday cake. It's like a slice of concentrated love with buttercream frosting."

— *Takayuki Ikkaku, Arisa Hosaka and Toshihiro Kawabata*

Having an "unbirthday" or special day for no reason other than to spend time together and break the routine can really bring you closer together and remind you of what is important.

Suggestions

- Choose a less hectic day and have an "unbirthday". Put up a couple of balloons, buy a cake and sing "Happy Unbirthday To Us"
- Have a 'We survived another day/week/month" party
- Choose a pet in the household to have a birthday for or a stuffed animal and go all out
- Celebrate "Us Day"; do something that celebrates who you are as a family and your accomplishments. Give out silly awards, have streamers, etc.
- If you can afford it, buy a gift for the family to open

Eat together every day

"Kids spell love T-I-M-E"

— *John Crudele*

Everyone has to eat and committing to eating together once a day (at least) is a great way of creating routine and consistency and touching base with each other as a family.

Suggestions
- Let everyone have some say in meal planning so that at least once a week they will be eating a meal they really love
- Have a set time for meals
- Plan around each person's weekly schedule to maximize the number of meals you can have together
- No text messaging, emailing, Blackberries, phone calls, etc. during dinner
- Put aside an hour for meals so they are not rushed events
- Plan meals ahead of time to reduce stress

Be predictable

"There must be consitency in direction"

— *W. Edwards Deming*

Do what you say and say what you mean. Follow through is not just part of a tennis or golf swing. The more predictable you are with your family the easier it is to predict their reactions and behaviour!

Suggestions

• Try to maintain routines like homework, meals, showers/baths as best as possible

• Follow through with consequences (even when you are tired as you will be exhausted having to suffer the consequences of not following through later on)

• If you are truly predictable you can ask your family what they think you are going to say and will probably give you the right answer

• Your family should know where you are and how they can easily get in touch with you

• Leave a work schedule, phone numbers of collegues, etc. for family to access

Knotted rope

"When you get to the
end of your rope, tie a
knot and hang on."

— *Franklin D. Roosevelt*

This is an unique way of counting down the days until your loved one is home.

Suggestions

- Tie as many knots as you are going to be away into a rope and each day someone in the family takes out another knot.
- Inside each knot write a note or a joke or a reassurance that can be read out
- Counting down the days is important but remember that flights and plans can change so always add a couple of knots and adjust accordingly closer to the date.
- Hang the rope somewhere everyone can see it regularly

Emergency Kits

"Be Prepared"

— Boy Scout Motto

(Robert Baden-Powell)

It is important to be prepared and organized for a variety of situations or events. Having kits or supplies "in case" can help alleviate worries or stress.

Suggestions

- Have a location in the house that is easily accessible to store batteries, candles, bottled water, can food, etc.
- Put a flash light in some frequently used rooms in the house
- Have a phone that isn't cordles that can be used during a power failure
- Battery powered or wind-up radio
- Prepare an emergency kit for the car – jumper cables, matches, candle, shovel, windshield washer fluid, etc.

Take pictures

"Life is not measured by the number of breaths we take, but by the moments that take our breath away"

— *Unknown*

Everyday take a picture that will tell a little something about your life at the moment or how your day went. It is another way of maintaining a log or journal of your lives while he/she is away that is quick and easy.

Suggestions

- Open up a folder to put each photo
- Date the photos so they can be seen in order
- Be creative
- Make sure you take a variety of pictures and include family whenever possible
- Have a family member create a caption for each photo
- Send the more creative or memorable photos to his/her email account whenever possible
- Create a slide slow for when they return

Screen Saver

"Missing someone gets easier everyday. Because, even though it is one day further from the last time you saw each other, it is one day closer to the next time you will"

— *Unknown*

Make a photo collage on the computer

and have it as your screen saver so that when you turn on your computer you are greeted with memorable or special photos.

Suggestions

- Ask people to send you their favourite or funniest photos (it is a good opportunity to get new/different photos from other people)
- Use photos that make you laugh, smile or remind you of something good or special
- Have a different screen saver for each month they are away
- Make a print of the screen saver for them to take when they are away or send the picture for them to use on their work computer or laptop

Family plans

"Great minds have purposes, others have wishes"

— *Washington Irving*

Creating a couple of basic plans for when things may not go as smoothly as you are hoping is not only a good idea but essential to ensure the safety of your family. Many of your previous plans may include the person who is away and who will be unable to provide immediate assistance or support.

Suggestions

- Who do you call if you are locked out?
- What do you do if you run out of gas?
- Who do you talk to if you hear gossip or rumours?
- Who would you call if you missed the bus?
- Where are the fire extinguishers? What do we do if there is a fire?
- What reasons would we call 911?
- What do you do if you forget your lunch/ homework/school things?

Reward

"The more you praise
and celebrate your life,
the more there is in life
to celebrate."

— *Oprah Winfrey*

For all things we do in life, there are rewards. Come up with appropriate ways of rewarding family members for their accomplishments. Remember that not all rewards need to have a monetary value.

Suggestions

- Reward a great day at school with their favourite dessert or meal
- Reward doing something without being asked with a hug and comment about how proud you are of them and why
- Reward getting out of bed and to school on time with a "Go to school late pass" or go our for breakfast together
- Reward getting homework completed on time with extra time on the computer, etc.
- Reward doing chores with a day off of doing them

Jokes & Quotes

"A day without laughter
is a day wasted"

— *Charlie Chaplin*

Start your day or week with humour or inspiration. Laughter really can be the best medicine.

Suggestions

- Subscribe to an internet site that will send you quotes or jokes
- Buy a calendar (and hang it in a high traffic area) that has jokes or inspirational thoughts or sentiments
- Make it a mission of each family member to take turns finding a joke or funny quote
- Put notes with jokes or cartoons on the fridge or in the cereal box each day or week
- Use funny, famous quotes to remimd everyone of the silly things people think and say

Jelly bean jar

"Count your smiles
instead of your tears;
count your courage
instead of your fears"

— *Unknown*

A fun way of keeping track of time passing during the absence is to eat jelly beans. Counting out jelly beans for each day the person is away can help children visually seeing time passing and they get to eat candy!

Suggestions

- Put a few extra in the jar in case of delays
- Put the jar in an easy to see area (that isn't as easy to access)
- If you eat from the jar, don't forget to replace them and label it so that other people don't eat them either
- Make it a part of your routine each day (Ex. After lunch or dinner, before brushing teeth each night, etc.)
- Make it a fun activity where the children make and decorate the jar
- If Jelly Beans are not a favourite use another type of candy or rasins, nuts, etc.

Create a log

> "I love sharing my story. It's endlessly healing."
>
> — *Ben Vereen*

As time passes the things you want to share or talk about change. Keeping a, "If you were here I'd tell you", log is a good way of expressing your thoughts and sharing them.

Suggestions

- Make a game of it at dinner and have each family member start with "If you were here I'd tell you…"
- Keep a blank sheet or book for everyone to jot their "If you were here's"
- Make a list of "If you were here" thoughts
- Ask family members to share what they think their reaction would be if they were there to hear it in person
- When their return is close, change it to "When you are here, I will…"

Create Top Ten Lists

"Twenty years from now you will be more disapointed by the things you didn't do then by the ones you did do."

— *Mark Twain*

Making top ten lists is an easy and fun way to talk as a family and a great way to document things that you were thinking, feeling or experiencing while they were away.

Suggestions

- Keep all of the lists in a book or journal
- Do one a day, week or month: whatever works for your family
- Top ten reasons why we miss you
- Top ten meals we have had while you were away
- Top ten things that annoy us
- Top ten things we have done since you have been away
- Top ten places we'd like to go on holidays
- Top ten things we are looking forward to
- Top ten favourite movies at the moment

Night-shirt

"Words of comfort, skillfully administered, are the oldest therapy known to man."

— *Louis Nizer*

Being able to wear the absent family member's shirt or item of clothing to bed can be comforting and give you a sense of a little part of them being with you.

Suggestions

• Choose something that is comfortable and was often worn so that helps you to remember the person and som fond memories of when they wore it

• Choose a t-shirt or something that will be easy to sleep in

• Have the person wear it, put paint on their hands and hug themselves with it on so that you will have the hug hand prints and each time you wear it (it will be like they are hugging you)

• Have their picture printed on the shirt

• Have them write some comforting thoughts or words onto the shirt

End conversations positively

"Each day comes bearing its own gifts, don't forget to untie the ribbons."

— *Ruth Ann Schabacker*

Ending each conversation on a positive note is important so that both parties can feel as though it is not all 'gloom and doom' and there are positive things happening or things to look forward to you do not want to put down the phone feeling worse then when it was picked up.

Suggestions

- Write down a list of good things that have happened and leave them by the phone
- End each call with a joke or phrase that will put a smile on each of your faces (Ex. It could be much worse, we could …)
- Re-affirm your love for each other
- Set a goal for each other that is simple and easy to accomplish for the next conversation
- Think before speaking

Make a placemat

"Other things may change us but we start and end with family."

— *Anthony Brandt*

Make a placemat with photos, sayings, your motto, etc. that can be used at each meal. They will help to enhance your meal times and add fun to your dinner table.

Suggestions

- Make them funny
- Have photos taken just before your family member leaves
- Everyone should have an opportunity to design at least one mat
- Add funny quotes, sayings, family mottos, jokes, designs, etc.
- Have them laminated for durability
- Get permanent marker for the back of the placemat and while they are away you can add things about what they ate, their day, special events, etc.

Create a pillow case

"Love is a canvas furnished by nature and embroidered imagination.

— *Voltaire*

Making a pillowcase for each family member will be a tremendous source of comfort each night as they get into bed.

Suggestions

- Have photos printed onto the pillow cases
- Put names, dates, loving comments, night time rituals/sayings, etc. on each pillow case
- Put hand or foot prints on pillow cases
- Write a poem or quote that will be a source of comfort
- Put dreams or wishes on the pillow

Introduce new activities

"Continuity does not rule out fresh approaches to fresh situations."

— *Dean Rusk*

Create a new family activity that you can do together while they are away and perhaps continue it when they come back. Creating new activities together empowers all family members.

Suggestions

- Choose an activity that is new to everyone so you can relate and grow with on another
- Buy and play a new game together (even if it is something you have no interest in)
- Start a family blog on the web
- Start a "night out" weekly or monthly and choose something that you
- Join a club or take a course together

Measure your children

"Things do not change, we change."

— *Henry David Thoreau*

Children grow and change like weeds and when you see them everyday it may not be as noticeable. To the family member away it will be amazing to follow their progress when they aren't there to see it themselves.

Suggestions

• Send their height in string and enclose it in each letter (if you have more than one child use different colours)

• Keep a chart at home and measure them monthly and mark it with their name and the date

• Keep a log of progress if they are doing something that may change their dreams, goals or appearance

• Take monthly photos and put the details on the back of the photo (be sure to take the photo in the same place, time of day, day of the month, outfit, etc. so that it is easy to spot the changes)

Clocks/Time charts

*"No matter how far appart we are
we look at the same moon and stars"*

—— *John Willman*

Having your family understand that you may not be doing the same things at the same times and why it may be difficult to contact each other is important. It is also an opportunity to teach them some geography!

Suggestions

- In a central room or each bedroom have two clocks (one for your time and for the time where the member of the family is)
- Make a time chart so that it is easy to read and have a rough idea of what the absent family member is doing at particular times of the day
- Before leaving the family could sit down and do a chart "When you are…. I am…"
- Make sure the clock has some way of indicating AM and PM

Make your own frames

"Memories are the welcome reprieve from the worries of my day."

— *Unknown*

Put framed pictures of your absent family member all over the house. Make your own frames with family to give the pictures further meaning.

Suggestions

- Buy photo mats and have your children put their finger prints all over the frame
- Have the family member leaving design some family photo frames for each member of the family's room to further personalize it
- Make frames for pictures to send so that it can easily be put up wherever they are
- Make a frame with family pictures and put some family saying or joke or quote in the middle of frame

Record your voice

"My mother had a beautiful, soothing voice that made me melt."

— *Gloria Estefan*

Hearing a loved one's voice can be comforting but also an opportunity to leave nothing unsaid.

Suggestions

- Go to a 'Build a Bear' type of store and use their voice recording in a stuffed toy to leave a special message they can play whenever they want
- Read stories onto a CD to listen to at night
- Create an alarm clock recording
- Record a CD that could be played on the way to work or school saying silly things, jokes, words of encouragement, etc.

Create scrapbooks

"There is more treasure in books than in all the pirates' loot on Treasure Island"

— *Walt Disney*

Keeping a scrapbook while your loved one is away is an excellent way of reflecting on your experiences and when reconnecting it is a good way to lay out what has happened in their absence and help them to 'fill in the gaps'.

Suggestions

- Put in photos, school notes, ticket stubs, etc.
- Add artwork or hand/footprints
- Have a page a week and put a couple of short notes about the week
- Ask other members of your family or friends to contribute
- If they are away for longer than a month: send them a scrapbook a month to keep them up to date
- Keep a box with the items you need to create the book so that it is easy to complete and find all of the items you need

Make a calendar together

"Family is not an important thing, it's everything."

— *Michael J. Fox*

Creating things to look forward to, organizing yourselves and including everyone in the process is a great way of making sure there is less stress and fewer misunderstandings.

Suggestions

- Sit down one night/day and look at the next 6 – 12 months (past the time of return, if possible)
- Add to the calendar special events, birthdays, anniversaries
- Put family goals, important meetings or obligations
- Plan for weekly family time
- Add a vacation or trip you can all do together
- Be sure to put on as many positive things and 'looking forward to' things as possible
- Put the calendar in a central location so that everyone can reference it (or add things to it) whenever they want to

Comfort blanket

"If you are cold at night, let the promise of my love cover you like a warm blanket."

— *Matthew White*

Having a blanket to go to bed with each night, not only provides you with warmth but memories too and can be a great way to end each day.

Suggestions

- Use his/her blanket as your own
- Take old clothing and make your own comforter or contact a local artisan and see if they can make one for you
- Have pictures printed onto a quilt of your family and of the person away so it is the last thing you see before falling asleep and the first thing you see waking up
- Contact a quilter and see if they could create something for you using materials that have significance and meaning to you both

clue a day

"Life is uncharted territory. It reveals its story one moment at a time."

— *Leo F. Buscaqlia*

Making the absence into an adventure for your family can often alleviate some stress and be a pleasant diversion for everyone.

Suggestions

- Children get a clue each day to find treasure
- They could have a map to create and add to each day
- Treasure could be discovered at different intervals depending on how long the person is away for
- Or children could make a clue for each day and then the parent has to go on a treasure hunt when they return

Hide pictures

"At the touch of love everyone becomes a poet."

— *Plato*

Everyone needs a 'boost' at unexpected times from someone they love. Take the time before the absence to take and hide pictures of your self and hide them in places where they will be found at different intervals.

Suggestions

- Put the pictures in different areas of your home (Ex. Christmas decorations, wrapping paper area, winter coats, etc.)
- Put the pictures in luggage so they will be discovered when unpacking/packing
- Hide pictures of yourself all over the house and write something on the back of each one
- Have the pictures reflect different holidays, emotions or sentiments

Make packages

"Love dosn't make the world go round. Love is what makes the ride worthwhile."

— *Franklin P. Jones*

With certain jobs or absences is it not always possible or easy to send packages back home. Making packages and pre-packaging them and organizing their postage at certain intervals may be helpful and a wonderful way to let children or significant others know that you love them and have thought of them.

Suggestions

- Have someone else mail them (if you are not able to)
- Add a personal note or letter that tells them about something about you and what you will be thinking about when they open it
- Include a map and mark where you will be or are at that time
- Get a little bit of currency from the country you are going to and include it
- Go on line and get a couple of books or CDs written or performed by people from the country or countries that you are going to
- Take a memory stick and send it back with photos on it for everyone to see where you are and what life for you is like

Video messages

"Goodnight stars goodnight air goodnight noises everywhere."

— *Margaret Wise Brown*

Having a personal greeting that can be played as part of a morning or evening routine would be a wonderful way of continuing to be a part of your family's daily life. Seeing you and hearing your voice will be comforting and a perfect way to start or end a day.

Suggestions
- Record yourself reading their favourite stories or a chapter of a novel each night
- Record a joke or thought for the day that they could play and have a different one each day
- Wish them good-night in at least 7 different ways so that there is a different good-night message for each day of the week
- Have some recorded messages for "in the event of…" (Ex. They have a great report card, homework isn't getting done, bad dream, scored a goal, etc.)

Give compliments

"A complement is verbal sunshine"

— *Robert Organ*

It is easy to think of all the things that you feel you aren't doing right and to get into a negative spiral when you are 'going it alone'. Make a conscientious effort everyday to give each family member a compliment and don't forget yourself!

Suggestions

- Each member of the family does it to another every day at dinner or breakfast
- It cannot be the same compliment each day
- Compliments must be meaningful and genuine
- Record compliments in a journal for yourself so that you can read through them and remember all the things you are getting right
- Make sure you are giving compliments at a family time that is not rushed

Create a family motto

"When you look at your life, the greates happines are family happinesses"

— *Dr. Joyce Brothers*

Having a creed or motto to live by can help a family to create a common focus or goal. It is good for everyone in a family to know what they all stand for as a family unit and can give each member a sense of pride in their family and its' beliefs.

Suggestions

- Look on the internet for company mottos for inspiration
- Think about the things that are important to your family and the beliefs that you share
- Make the motto simple and easy to remember
- Have a plaque made with it on and place it somewhere it can be seen everyday as a reminder to everyone
- Research your family's heritage for ideas

Getting information

"It is only because of problems that we grow mentally and spiritually"

— *M. Scott Peck*

Don't listen to sensationalized media reports or idle gossip. Make sure that you know who and how to access up-to-date and accurate information. Have addresses and contact information readily available.

Suggestions

- Get all contact information <u>before</u> they leave
- Give the contact information to family, neighbours or close friend
- Avoid listening to media reports that may be sensationalized or exaggerated
- Find official and reliable source to receive information and news
- Keep a list of useful contacts and/or email addresses on the fridge
- Cancel your newspaper subscription if it upsets you, and subscribe to a magazine you would enjoy reading

Phone messages

"In times of test,
family is best."

— *Burmese proverb*

Hearing a person's voice can be soothing for everyone in the family. Save messages at least until everyone in the family has heard it and create ones that will leave a smile.

Suggestions

• For the person who is away - make sure that you are leaving a message that is positive and that you wouldn't mind everyone hearing or indicate otherwise.

• When leaving messages make sure you indicate when you may possibly call again

• Record a message greeting that is fun and even put a coded type of message into it for the absent family member to enjoy hearing if they aren't going to be able to speak to you in person

• Make sure you can save your messages and if not contact your local phone company to find out if it is a feature you can add

Making Decisions

"Good plans shape good decisions"

— *Anonymous*

Include absent family member in as many decisions as possible. Ask ahead of time what kinds of things they would like to be consulted on. The absent family member must also remember that sometimes there is not the luxury of time to wait for their input and decisions have to be made.

Suggestions

• Arrange in advance what types of things the absent family member would consider important to be consulted on

• Talk about different scenarios that may occur in their absence and what you would do

• Have a phone code when you want to communicate privately without anyone else on the line

• Have an agreed upon list of people that could be contacted to consult with that everyone thinks makes good judgments, gives good advice and usually makes good suggestions

• Avoid regret and remember that you did the best you could with the support and information you had at the time

• Talk openly and honestly with all those that will be effected or involved

Mapping their journey

"Life isn't about waiting for the storm to pass. It's about learning to dance in the rain"

— *Anonymous*

Chart or map their travels. If it is possible, make it a family activity and keep track of their adventure or experience. It is educational and can help facilitate conversation.

Suggestions

• Give everyone in the family an opportunity to learn some geography by taking turns mapping out the journey or possible journey(s).

• Get a world map and mark on the map the different towns, cities, states/provinces, countries or continents that your loved one is going to or has been.

• Do some research about where they are and even cook a meal that would be common for people of that region to eat.

• Talk about how long it takes to get there, what types of transportation is possible, etc.

Homework

"Education is not filling a bucket but, lighting a fire"

— *William Butler Yeats*

Homework is a part of life. Your child's job is to go to school every day and do their best. If they made good use of school time, asked for help when they needed it and are organized there should be no more than 30 minutes to 1 hour per night of homework.

Suggestions

- If your child has more than 45 minutes a night of homework, call and speak to the teacher – during an absence children need time to relax and unwind as well
- Put homework into your family's nightly routine
- Choose a quiet location with good lighting
- No phone calls, MSN, TV or other distractions for this period
- If they have no homework they can read or organize binders and notes – keeping the routine is essential
- Use a desk and comfortable chair
- Check in on progress regularly but try not to hover
- Have clear and consistent rewards when homework time is complete and consequences when time is not used productively

Money Jar

> "An aim in life is the only fortune worth finding."
>
> — *Jacqueline Kennedy Onassis*

Put a set amount of money in a jar for each day they are away and then spend it on frivolous or fun things when you are all back together.

Suggestions

- Have a jar out on the table where everyone can see it
- Let everyone in the family know the purpose for your jar
- Have everyone make a list of all the things that they would like to spend the money on
- Determine together the amount of money to put into the jar each day
- Do a weekly/monthly count so that even the youngest members of your family can understand how much is in there and what is possible and not possible

Learn new things

"Education is not filling a
bucket but, lighting a fire"

—— *William Butler Yeats*

Taking the time to learn new things or 'expand your horizons' will not only keep you busy but also allow you to experience new things while your absent family member is doing the same thing! When you are together again, you will both have new experiences to share.

Suggestions

- Go to library or local bookstore or online and order a few books you have wanted to read for awhile
- Sign up for a evening or weekend course in something you love or are really interested in learning or doing
- Take swimming, skiing, yoga, pottery, dance, etc. lessons
- Visit an art gallery, museum, historical site, etc. each week/month
- Encourage family members to join you or do their own thing too

Phone calls

> "Yesterday is but today's memory and tomorrow is today's dream."
>
> — *Kahlil Bibran*

Things will come up and you will say 'I wish I could ask him/her about that…" and then you will get your phone call and forget all about it! Take notes or make a list of things that you want to ask about or tell them about and leave it on the fridge, by the phone or in a place where you will know where to find it quickly.

Suggestions

• Get a book for this sole purpose and keep it beside your bed or in your purse or in the car (wherever you can access it regularly and easily)

• Also write down important accomplishments or successes achieved so that you are also relaying positive information

• Prioritize the list so that you ask the most important things first, especially if there is a limit to how long you are going to be able to talk for

• Read the list over again daily as some of your questions may become redundant or unnecessary and would waste valuable time

Send Flowers

"A bit of fragrance clings to the hand that gives flowers."

— Chinese Proverb

Sending a bouquet of flowers at a special time or just as a "pick-me-up" can help reduce feelings of isolation, loneliness sadness or just say an "I love you" at the right time.

Suggestions

• Get the names and contact information of several florists in your area or in the areas of extended family
• Set up an account with a local florist
• Pick dates and plan deliveries in advance
• Remember dates like Valentines Day, Mother's Day, birthdays, anniversaries, etc.
• Write the cards accompanying the delivery in advance

"A day in the life of…"

"The only difference between a good day and a bad day is your attitude."

— *Dennis Brown*

Keeping a log (video, email or letter) of a day helps everyone to gain a unique perspective on how things are on a daily basis for each other even when they are apart. You can often get into the mode of thinking that your life is harder, more stressful, boring, exciting, etc. than the other person's.

Suggestions

- Write or record, on a typical day, all of the things you do, experience, people you meet, tasks you have, etc.
- Don't leave out the menial tasks as they are often important too
- Write or record it as factually as possible and leave out opinions so that your family can just see or read about your day without being influenced by your feelings or perceptions
- Be as detailed as possible, what you find silly or boring may be of interest to your family or friends
- Each family member could participate in this activity which will help later on when your family is reuniting

Plant a seed

"There are no such things as limits to growth, because there are no limits to the human capacity for intelligence, imagination, and wonder."

— *Ronald Reagan*

Just like you grow in their absence, so will a plant and there is no better way to show children that they change and grow like the seed they planted.

Suggestions

- Plant a seed in the garden or in a pot in the house (climate dependent)
- Talk about how and when it grows and what it needs to thrive
- Measure it regularly, take photos of it or keep a log you can share when they get back
- Compare the plant's grow with your children(s)'s growth
- Talk about growth you can see and the growth that happened inside too

A time to think

"Love does not consist of gazing at each other but in looking outward together in the same direction"

— *Antoine de Saint-Exupery*

A tremendous source of comfort can be in knowing that someone is thinking of and missing you as much as and at the same time as you are thinking of them.

Suggestions

• Make an easy and realistic time that can easily be worked into your routine

• Read the book "Night Catch" by Brenda Ehrmantraut to younger children about a military man who has to go away but plays with his son each night with the stars

• Put an alarm on each of your watches for a certain time of the day and when it goes off you know you are thinking of each other

• Send a text once a day that simply says "Right now I am missing you" or some other personal greeting

Breakfast for dinner

"Food is the most primative
form of comfort"

— *Sheila Graham*

Not only is having breakfast for dinner sometimes a simple dinner solution but children love the idea of mixing up things a little and it can make for a meal filled with smiles and laughter.

Suggestions

- Ask your children what day of the week they would like to do it on
- Get a toast stamp that has a funny greeting you can stamp into their toast
- Pour the pancake mix into large cookie cutter shapes
- Make a smoothie or punch to go with it
- Use fun paper plates or fancy dishes to make it different and special
- Eat in a different room of your house (dinning room, living room on the carpet, out on the deck, on a blanket in the backyard, etc.)

Support groups

"The more you lose yourself in something bigger than yourself, the more energy you will have."

—— *Norman Vincent Peale*

Getting together with friends or people in similar situations can provide you with an outlet to share your feelings, frustrations, stresses, etc. and help you to realize that you are normal and that other people feel the exact same way!

Suggestions

- Contact support agencies to inquire about local supports
- Ask at your family's church
- If military, contact your local military family resource centre or support centre
- See your doctor for a referral or suggestions
- Ask friends or colleagues

Get a babysitter

"A good film is when the price of the dinner, the theatre admission and the babysitter were worth it."

— *Alfred Hitchcock*

Get a reliable babysitter whom you trust and can ask to help on a regular basis. This can really help you to maintain your sanity and give you the time away from some of your daily/nightly responsibilities that you need and deserve.

Suggestions

- Ask around your neighbourhood
- Be direct with your babysitter about when you will need her, what type of person you are (always last minute, late, early, on time, unpredicatable)
- Have a set time each week when you know he/she is available <u>and use it</u>
- Try to have more than one babysitter as they have lives too and may not be available when you really need it so having a back-up means you can get the time you need
- Pay a little extra (it doesn't have to be a lot but find out what the going rate is and pay a little more — it tells your babysitter you think she/he is worth it and can assure that they will be more likely to say yes to you!)
- Be clear with your expectations and say them in front of your children so that everyone is aware and on the 'same page'

Call display

> "I believe that you should gravitate to people who are doing productive and positive things with their lives."

— *Nadia Comaneci*

There are times when you don't have the time, energy, desire, etc. to talk to people and having call display allows you to prioritize but also manage your time more efficiently. This also allows you to avoid telemarketers that can be demanding and take up time and energy you don't have.

Suggestions

- Take note of when people have called and commit to getting back to the person within a certain time frame
- Let people know there are certain times you are not going to answer the phone and that if it is an emergency call back immediately (a second call in a row would mean it is urgent)
- Having call display also means you won't miss the calls you really want to get no matter what the time is!
- Call up your local phone company and ask them to tell you about all the possible package options so that you can have the best possible service for the best price (if you do not wish to continue these services once your family member has returned make sure you are not locked into this plan for a set amount of time or that there aren't penalties for ending it)

Create a blog

"Communiction is depositing a part of yourself in another person."

— *Anonymous*

The online world is quick and anyone can access it with the touch of a few keys (from anywhere in the world). A blog can be a fun and quick way of letting everyone know how you are doing during the absence.

Suggestions

- It is not secure so do not put anything up on a blog that you wouldn't want the whole world to know about
- Be careful with the pictures you put up as anyone can access them
- Don't let updating the blog become another bothersome task, if your children are older let them help and be a significant contributor
- Make a set time in the day/week to do it and limit your self to a few minutes a day or week
- Let everyone know that you when you update it and what to expect, reminding them of your limits

> "Don't pray for lighter burdens, but for stronger backs."

— *Phillips Brooks*

Pray 90

Many people find comfort in prayer.

Make time for your self each day, week, month to reflect on your life, your loves and your God.

Suggestions

- If you enjoy attending services or prayer meetings/groups, keep doing it
- Let people know that this is important to you and you will be taking time out to do this
- Find comfort with those that have the same beliefs as you
- Talk about the prayers of others to remind yourself of other people's needs, lives and sufferings
- Make attending services or prayer groups a priority

Listen to music

"Music washes away from the soul the dust of everyday life."

— *Berthold Auerbach*

Music has the ability to make you feel happy, sad, reflective, etc. It can bring back happy memories and lift you up when you need it.

Suggestions

- Make two identical CDs of your favourite songs so that you will each have a copy to listen to
- Make CDs or put onto your MP3 player songs for different moods
- Have music for different times of the day or occasions (working out, birthday party, going to bed)
- Send each other songs to listen to that you like or provoked a feeling or mood

Go to the spa

"The way you treat yourself sets the standards for others"

— *Sonya Friedman*

Treat yourself every now and again. You deserve it! Letting someone else pamper you and help you to feel beautiful or relaxed is worth more than you would believe.

Suggestions

- Get a different haircut
- Get a massage or reflexology treatment
- Ask a friend to join you for a pedicure or manicure
- Book at a place that has been recommended to you and you've always wanted to go
- If you don't want the added stress or expense of a babysitter look into have a home visit and invite some friends over and make a party out of it
- Book it in advance and let your family know this is important to you

Re-decorate

"Variety is the soul of pleasure"

— *Aphra Behn*

Changing a room can change your mood and give you a sense of accomplishment and positive change. Don't take on too much but some simple changes can be just the boost you need.

Suggestions

- Decide on a budget
- Plan it out carefully and make sure you have enough time to get it done without being overwhelmed
- Ask other people to come and help
- Try not to take on too many new tasks as you are not always sure how long they will take and you don't want to end up consumed by the project
- Seek professional advice, even if you don't use it, it is good to get perspectives from others that have done it before and may have some time and money saving suggestions you hadn't thought of
- Add 2 hours to each task and that way even if you are on time and didn't need it you now have time planned for that you can use for yourself

Volunteer

"Real generosity toward the future lies in giving all to the present."

— *Albert Camus*

Doing things for others is gratifying. It can change the lives of others whilst also providing you with some routine, a sense of accomplishment and giving that extends into other parts of your life.

Suggestions

- Don't take on big tasks that will take up too much of your time, leaving you no time for yourself
- Do something that you like
- Choose something that interests you
- Try it out before making any solid commitments
- Have a good look at your schedule and make sure that what you are doing will fit in with your life and time commitments
- Do some research and find out what organizations are in your area and need assistance

Record events

"I always laugh the hardest at the stuff you see in day-to-day life."

— *Luke Wilson*

Borrowing or getting a reasonable priced and user friendly video recorder for important events, significant moments and even day to day goings on would help bridge the gaps when the family member returns or while they are away.

Suggestions

- At larger gatherings with family and friends video messages that all start with — "We wish you were here because…"
- Make sure you are able to use the video recorder properly and if not, that you have someone available and close by that can help you navigate through it
- Remember to not always be the one doing the recording, give it to many different people to record as they will focus on different things and there would also be video of you in it as well

Plan a vacation

"You have to have a dream
so you can get up in the
morning."

— *Billy Wilder*

Planning a family vacation or holiday gives everyone something to focus on and look forward to once the family is reunited. Make sure everyone is aware of the plans, budget and the reason for the holiday.

Suggestions

- Look at your budget and make a savings plan
- Before booking make sure you have spoken to someone who has experience with the type or location of your holiday so that your family is aware of what to expect
- Have everyone in the family write down their holiday 'to do' priorities
- Before inviting extended family or others on the holiday, check with everyone first
- Check on your government website for travel restrictions or requirements if you are leaving the country
- Make sure you have appropriate insurance and documentation

Use the fancy dishes

"You can't depend on your eyes if your imagination is out of focus. "

— *Mark Twain*

Putting a different 'spin' on mealtimes can sometimes be the thing that puts everyone in an upbeat frame of mind. Get out the special dishes and don't cook a thing. Order take out and even have it delivered!

Suggestions

- Have it on a night when everyone will be home for dinner
- Do it on a night when you have lots of time
- Have everyone agree on what you are ordering
- Order it a day in advance (most take out places like to have advanced orders so they can plan better too) so that you don't have any planning and could pick up on the way home
- Get out the seasonal or fancy dishes to make it special and fun

Make up a holiday

"You are only given a little spark of madness. You mustn't lose it."

— *Robin Williams*

G

ive yourself a reason to bring some fun and silliness into your home and family! Invent a special holiday that you can celebrate together and do something unusual or special or just spend time together.

Suggestions

- Keep it simple, don't add to your load and remember that the number one thing that makes family happy is when you give them your undivided attention
- Name your holiday
- Record your celebrations so that they can be shared when everyone is together again
- Get a cake or favourite dessert and indulge your family
- Blow up balloons, get a door banner or decorate in some fun way

Acknowledge dates

"Thousands of candles can be lit from a single candle, and the life of the candle will not be shortened. Happiness never decreases by being shared"
— *Buddha Quote (Hindu Prince Gautama Siddharta, 563-483BC)*

Remembering important dates and acknowledging them is important. You may not all be together to celebrate or recognize an important or significant date or event but by having something prepared you can let people know you've thinking of them.

Suggestions

• Take a shoe box and put dividers into it for each month, buy cards ahead of time and have them ready to send for birthdays and anniversaries, congratulations, etc.

• If they are away on their birthday have a cake and a special dinner without them and film it (send them the video if possible)

• For each week or month that goes by have a special ritual, dinner, breakfast, night out to say "We survived"

• Ask a neighbour or friend to hold on to the gifts or cards, etc. and deliver them on the correct day.

• Pre-arrange deliveries/orders (gift, flowers, etc.)

Praise Yourself

"Courage is the most important of all virtues, because without it we can't practice any other virtue with consistency"

— *Maya Angelou*

P raise yourself and your ability to make it even in the absence of a significant family member. It takes inner strength, courage and character to not just survive but thrive during the absence. Everyday find something to congratulate your self on.

Suggestions

- Before starting your day think about something you did the day before that was successful or worked out
- Write down each day a thing that you are good at or that you are proud of
- Accept compliments that others give you and write them down
- Read over your lists or notes regularly to remind your self of all the good things about your self and the things you have accomplished
- Don't compare your accomplishments or hardships to others
- Create a mantra for yourself each day (ex. I am courageous and strong, I will not only survive this experience, I will be stronger and able to handle anything that comes my way)

Read this Book

"One of the things I learned the hard way was that it doesn't pay to get discouraged. Keeping busy and making optimism a way of life can restore your faith in yourself."

— *Lucille Ball*

Notes:

Notes:

Notes: